TEST YOUR O

MW01105147

Spelling

B. A. Phythian

Headway · Hodder & Stoughton

This Headway edition first published 1990
by Hodder and Stoughton Educational,
a division of Hodder and Stoughton Ltd,
Mill Road, Dunton Green, Sevenoaks, Kent.

ISBN 0 340 52719 6

Printed and bound in Great Britain by CW Print Group, Loughton, Essex.

Contents

Before you begin

The most important words in this book are always printed in green. All these words must always be learnt, using the rules you are given on this page.

To use this book, you will need a dictionary.

You will also need a notebook. Write A at the top of the first page, B at the top of the second, and so on through the alphabet. When you are asked to write down a word, look at the first letter of the word and write it on the page which has the same letter at the top. In this way you will build up your own Spelling Dictionary. You can write in any other words you come across which you didn't know before, but don't write them in until you've found out what they mean.

Always learn to spell all the words you write down.

1 Look at them carefully.
2 Cover them up (or close your eyes) and spell them out aloud to yourself.
3 Check that you've got them right. (If you haven't, start again.)
4 Write them on a piece of paper.
5 Ask someone to test you.
6 When you're quite sure you know them, write them in your own Spelling Dictionary.

It's more fun if you keep a record of your score. After a week or two, try the same exercise again and see if you can get a better score. If you get a worse one, you need to learn the exercise again!

There's no substitute for hard learning – over and over and over again.

Do you know these meanings? You will need to know them for this book.

vowel – the letters **a**, **e**, **i**, **o** and **u**. The letter **y** can also be used as a vowel.

consonant– the other letters of the alphabet.

syllable – a sound containing a vowel with or without consonants. The word **elm** has one syllable; **asleep** has two syllables (**a**- and **-sleep**); **elastic** has three (**e-las-tic**); **education** has four (**e-duc-a-tion**).

1 Words with qu

The letter **q** is always followed by **u** and a vowel. **qu** nearly always makes the sound **kw**. You seldom find words containing **-kw-** (you never find **kw** at the beginning of a word), so if a word has the sound **kw** it will usually be spelt with **qu**.

request	quality	squander	squeeze	squint
enquire	quantity	quarter	question	quote
quiet	quarry	quaint	square	require

There are a few words in which **qu** makes the sound **k**:

quay	picturesque	unique	conquer	grotesque

There is one word in which **qu** makes a different sound: **queue**

Fill in the gaps in the words. Don't forget to learn the completed words.

A person who knows someone is said to be **acq_ _ inted** with him.
Athletes always have a good **ph_si_ _ _.**
A **_ _ _z** is a test of knowledge.
Pigs **sq_ _ _ l**, ducks **_ _ a_ k** and mice **sq_ _ ak**.
You may **q_ _ n_ _** your thirst by drinking orange **_q_ _ _ _.**
Here are some words you may use in geography: earth **_ _ _k_,**
eq_ _ tor.
Instead of money, you can use a **ch_ _ _ e.**

Look in your dictionary to find the difference between

quay, key	queue, cue	conquer, conker

Puzzle corner

All the words in this list can be pronounced in two different ways with two different meanings. What are they?

read	wind	lead	refuse	rebel	permit
tear	close	minute	excuse	object	present

2 Words with **gh**

The letters **gh** are sometimes silent:

ought	fright	height	weigh	through
bought	high	night	caught	although
straight	flight	bright	neigh	taught
thought	slightly	lightning	eight	plough

Sometimes **gh** sounds like **f**:

enough	cough	laugh	laughter
rough	draught	tough	toughness

Sometimes **gh** sounds like **g** (usually at the beginning of words):

ghastly	ghost	ghostly

g on its own is sometimes silent, too:

sign	reign	foreign	campaign	gnash	gnaw

Write in your Spelling Dictionary a word that rhymes with

thorough	and means a town with its own government
fight	and means a difficult situation
naughty	and means too proud
daughter	and means killing
sigh	and means the upper part of the leg
sight	and means the opposite of left
fought	and means nothing
might	and means the opposite of loose
plough	and means part of a tree

If you have learnt the words on this page, you should also be able to spell

frightful	nightfall	brightly	twilight	neighbour
frightening	nightmare	brightness	weighing	eighteen
frightened	fortnight	thoughtful	weight	eighty
roughly	draughty	sovereign	foreigner	though

3 Words with **w** and **wh**

There are not many spelling problems with the **w** sound in English. Here are some **w** words that you will need to know:

window	weaken	wealthy	weapon	winter
wield	worse	wisdom	wishful	world
worth	wilderness	wasteful	worried	welcome
weary	Wednesday	warrior	watch	wonderful

However, there are a few words in which the **w** sound is spelt **wh**. You will already know the common ones:

what	when	where	which	while	why

It is also important to know these words:

whisper	whistle	white	whip	wheel
whine	whimper	whirl	whisker	wheat

Unscramble these mixed-up **wh** words and decide which of the definitions they match:

rawfh	ehwzee	fwfhi	nehiw	khwis	hkcaw

1 faint smell
2 place where ships load and unload
3 sharp blow
4 kitchen utensil
5 complaining sound
6 breathe with difficulty

Use your dictionary to find the difference between

whine, wine	which, witch	whether, weather	whole, hole

Puzzle corner

Here are some words that sound the same but have different spellings. Look in your dictionary to make sure you understand them.

knew, new	past, passed	check, cheque
peace, piece	led, lead	stationary, stationery

4 Words ending in **-ant** and **-ance**

Make sure you understand these words, then learn them:

pleasant	giant	nuisance	advance	performance
instant	vacant	balance	attendance	ambulance
inhabitant	constant	vengeance	admittance	disturbance

Some words ending in **-ant** can also end in **-ance**:

assistant, assistance	extravagant, extravagance
important, importance	significant, significance
ignorant, ignorance	reluctant, reluctance

Change the following words to end in **-ance**. Write both forms of the word in your Spelling Dictionary.

defiant	fragrant	abundant	elegant	entrant

Some **-ant** words cannot end in **-ance**, but they can end in **-ation**. Copy out these words in your Spelling Dictionary, then write them out with the ending **-ation.**

applicant	indignant	occupant	consultant

Write out the following words with the correct ending, **-ance** or **-ence**:

griev _ _ _ _	audi _ _ _ _	appear _ _ _ _	refer _ _ _ _
confer _ _ _ _	disappear _ _ _ _	acquaint _ _ _ _	annoy _ _ _ _

Puzzle corner

Here are some words that children – and grown-ups – often spell wrongly. Learn them very carefully.

definitely	immediately	separate	believe
receive	already	develop	parliament
parallel	all right	grammar	benefited

5 Plurals

Most words form the plural by adding **-s**:

surprise, surprises   **depth, depths**   **limit, limits**

Words ending in **-ch**, **-o**, **-s**, **-sh**, **-ss**, **-x**, and **-z** add **-es**:

sandwich, sandwiches	**hero, heroes**
polish, polishes	**glass, glasses**
bus, buses	**volcano, volcanoes**
fox, foxes	**success, successes**

But several useful words ending in **-o** simply add **-s** in the plural:

photos   pianos   studios   zoos   radios   cuckoos   twos

Words ending in **-f** or **-fe** change the **-f** or **-fe** to **-ves**:

knife, knives   thief, thieves   shelf, shelves   loaf, loaves

except for

chief, chiefs   proof, proofs   belief, beliefs   roof, roofs
cliff, cliffs

You can please yourself with

scarfs or **scarves   handkerchiefs** or **handkerchieves   hoofs** or **hooves**

Think of five words ending in **-o** and meaning something you might

1 load on to a ship (**c _ _ _ _**)
2 fry (**p _ t _ _ _**)
3 grow in a greenhouse (**t _ m _ _ _**)
4 play with (**_ o _ _ n _**)
5 hear coming back (**_ _ _ _**)

Think of five words ending in **-f** and meaning something you might

1 turn over newly (**_ _ _ _**)
2 read about seven of (**_ _ _ _ _**)
3 keep from the door (**w _ _ _**)
4 double into a whole (**_ _ _ _**)
5 do-it-? (**_ _ _ _ _ _ _ _**)

Write both the singular and plural forms of the words in your Spelling Dictionary.

6   More plurals

To form the plural of words ending in **-y**, change the **y** into **i** and add **es**, but only if the letter before the **-y** is a consonant:

family, families	discovery, discoveries	factory, factories
country, countries	enemy, enemies	hobby, hobbies
memory, memories	injury, injuries	victory, victories

If the letter before the **-y** is a vowel, just add **s** to form the plural:

chimney, chimneys   valley, valleys   holiday, holidays

Some words are the same in the singular and the plural:

salmon   sheep   aircraft   deer   cod

To make it really complicated, some things have no singular:

scissors   pants   goods   riches   thanks   trousers

Some words make the plural in special ways:

child, children	mouse, mice	woman, women	crisis, crises
tooth, teeth	goose, geese	man, men	foot, feet

Using these rules, and the ones on the previous page, write out the plurals of

mystery	birthday	tooth	church	robbery	yourself
donkey	match	wife	lorry	beach	cowboy

Use your dictionary to find the difference between

storey, story

Write down the plurals of these two words in your Spelling Dictionary.

Puzzle corner

Here are some words that sound nearly alike, but have different spellings. Make sure you understand the differences.

loose, lose	chose, choose	quite, quiet
accept, except	advice, advise	hoarse, horse

7 Words ending in consonant + y

If a word ends in -**y** and there is a consonant immediately in front of the -**y**, you must change the -**y** into **i** if you want to add an ending.

easy, easily   thirty, thirtieth   copy, copies
happy, happiness,   happily, happier   dry, drier, dried, dries
beauty, beautiful

Can you think of other endings for these words?

The rule does not apply if you want to add the ending -**ing**. Then you keep the **y**:

supply, supplying   satisfy, satisfying   fortify, fortifying

The rule does not apply in a few other cases also:

shy, shyness, shyly   sly, slyness, slyly   dry, dryness

Add -**ing** and -**ed** to these words, and write them in your Spelling Dictionary:

occupy   terrify   empty   study   hurry   rely
marry   spy   worry   tidy   reply   accompany

Add -**ly** to these words, and write them in your Spelling Dictionary:

steady   angry   busy   clumsy   hungry   unlucky
cheeky   shabby   temporary   weary   noisy   stealthy

Add -**ness** to these words, and write them in your Spelling Dictionary:

heavy   busy   clumsy   weary   untidy   lovely
lonely   silly   empty   ugly   juicy   nasty

Puzzle corner

Here is another list of words that are often mis-spelt. Learn them thoroughly.

till, until   recognise   humorous   actually
embarrass   because   awkward   although
fulfil   library   particularly   necessary

8 More words ending in -y

If a word ends in **y** and there is a vowel immediately in front of the **-y**, you do not change the **-y** if you want to add an ending:

buy, buyer, buying   **play, playful, playing**

But there are a few special **-ay** words which you ought to learn:

day, daily   **gay, gaily, gaiety**
pay, paid (but **pays, paying, payment**)   **lay, laid** (but **lays, laying**)
say, said (but **saying, says**)

Read these sentences:

I arrived **early**.   He arrived **earlier**.   They arrived **earliest** of all.

Now add **-er** and **-est** to these words:

clumsy	lazy	nasty	lively	juicy	gloomy
holy	shabby	silly	sturdy	flimsy	dreary
tidy	easy	cosy	dry	busy	heavy

Learn and write the plurals of these words:

body	remedy	mystery	apology	monkey
century	casualty	holiday	misery	activity
journey	ally	railway	library	jelly
convoy	industry	anxiety	army	lorry
party	difficulty	memory	robbery	lady

Add **-ment**, **-ous**, or **-ful** to these words:

victory	enjoy	glory	employ	mercy
accompany	play	study	merry	mystery

Correct these sentences. Make sure you understand why they are wrong!

It never reigns but it pores.
The reins in Spain fall mainly on the plane.
He herd the sound of slay-bells.
How much do you way?
I knocked in vein.
Weight a moment, your heir needs combing.
Patients is a virtue.
The peer was washed away by heavy seize.

9 Looks different, sounds the same: **ch** and **tch**

In English, the same sound can be made by different letters or groups of letters. For example, the final sound in **touch** is the same as in **clutch**, but you see that one is spelt with **ch** and the other with **tch**.

The same sound in the middle of **archway** and **kitchen** is also spelt differently.

There are no rules to help you, but here are some useful examples to learn:

ch *at the beginning*		**ch** *in the middle*		**ch** *at the end*	
cheerful	chocolate	mischief	treacherous	brooch	launch
champion	charity	purchase	merchant	scorch	search

There are no English words beginning with **tch**, but look carefully at **tch** in

scratched	patchwork	switches	fetching	stitch
pitches	match	sketches	snatch	stretch

Fill the spaces in these words with **ch** or **tch** and write the complete words in your Spelling Dictionary:

ca__   tor__   dispa__ed   trun__eon   __alk   deta__ed   clen__

10 Looks the same, sounds different: **ch**

In this list, **ch** sounds like **k**:

chaos	Christmas	anchor	mechanic	stomach	architect
chorus	chemist	ache	orchestra	choir	scheme

Which of the words from this list mean

1 disorder, confusion
2 plan
3 designer of buildings

4 person who repairs machinery
5 the same as another word in the list

Sometimes **ch** sounds like **sh**:

machine	chivalry	crochet	schedule	moustache

Can you think of four words beginning **ch** (but pronounced **sh**) meaning

1 an expensive fizzy wine
2 an ornamental light-holder

3 the framework of a car
4 a Swiss house

11 Words ending in -er and -ar

Many English words end in **-er**:

customer	shelter	embroider	weather	shower
hammer	chapter	messenger	shoulder	prayer
frontier	helicopter	remember	passenger	register

The **-ar** ending sounds the same, but is less common:

calendar	popular	vulgar	grammar	burglar
singular	solar	peculiar	regular	similar
collar	familiar	particular	sugar	dollar

Fill in the squares with a word which describes someone who

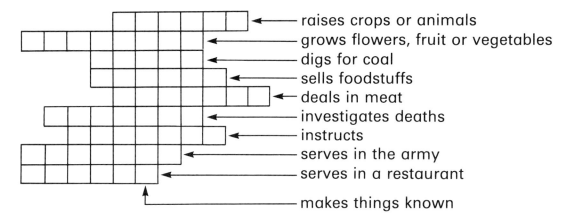

raises crops or animals
grows flowers, fruit or vegetables
digs for coal
sells foodstuffs
deals in meat
investigates deaths
instructs
serves in the army
serves in a restaurant
makes things known

Use your dictionary to find the difference between

border, boarder	pillar, pillow	weather, whether
boulder, bolder	meter, metre	alter, altar

Puzzle corner

Change one letter in the words printed in green to make them fit the definitions:

cellar	– worn round the neck	nettle	– utensil for boiling water
gallop	– quantity of liquid	cuddle	– crowd together
swallow	– not deep	muddle	– small pool
chatter	– break in pieces	raffle	– confuse, puzzle
flutter	– praise	marriage	– vehicle

12   Words with -or and -our

The **-or** and **-our** endings sound like the **-er** and **-ar** ones.

corridor	error	survivor	ancestor	mirror
radiator	visitor	traitor	motor	tractor
colour	favour	armour	vapour	harbour
flavour	rumour	behaviour	endeavour	splendour

In some words, **our** sounds different.

journey   courage   tournament   devour   detour   ourselves

Notice an important change if you want to add **-ous** to words ending in **-our**:

humour, but humorous   vigour, but vigorous
glamour, but glamorous   labour, but laborious

Write out these words and then write out their feminine forms:

actor   author   mayor   emperor   conductor

Write out these words and then write out their opposites:

major   exterior   junior   inferior   predecessor

Fill in the squares with a word which describes someone who

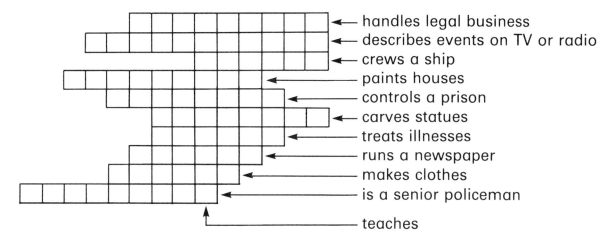

←— handles legal business
←— describes events on TV or radio
←— crews a ship
←— paints houses
←— controls a prison
←— carves statues
←— treats illnesses
←— runs a newspaper
←— makes clothes
←— is a senior policeman
←— teaches

Use your dictionary to find the difference between

morning, mourning   our, hour

Write out these numbers in words: 4, 14, 40, 44.

13   Words with **au** and **ua**

The letters **au** usually sound like **or**:

| applause | automatic | precaution | saucer | authority |

But they can make other sounds. Say these words out loud and learn them:

| because | laughter | gauge | beautiful | cauliflower |
| sausage | aunt | draught | bureau | chauffeur |

The letters **ua** usually sound as they do in

| actual | continual | individual | punctual | situated |

except after **q**.

ua can make various other sounds, too:

| persuade | language | truant | guard | guarantee |

It is important to learn these words very thoroughly.

14   Words ending in **-ure**

In many words, the ending **-ure** sounds like the endings **-er**, **-ar**, **-or**, and **-our**.

| figure | injure | measure | conjure | pressure | exposure |

This is also true of **-ure** words ending in **-ture**, which sounds like **cher**:

venture	temperature	torture	signature	capture
creature	lecture	nature	manufacture	puncture
future	picture	fixture	adventure	agriculture

But some **-ure** endings sound like **your** or **sure**:

| mature | endure | obscure | assure | insure | unsure |

Write in your Spelling Dictionary words ending in **-ure** which mean the same as:

1 wealth; something precious, highly valued
2 stories, plays, poetry
3 lack of success
4 chairs, tables, beds
5 area for grazing
6 joy, satisfaction, happiness

15 Looks different, sounds the same: endings -le, -al, -el

Here are more words with similar sounds but different spellings:

words ending in -le		words ending in -al		words ending in -el	
sparkle	middle	natural	typical	quarrel	panel
vehicle	article	original	practical	parcel	rebel
grumble	trouble	several	hospital	level	model
obstacle	people	special	usual	marvel	fuel

Finish off these words, using -le, -al, or -el.
Check in a dictionary to make sure you're right.

loy _ _	start _ _	capit _ _	post _ _	circ _ _
di _ _	sign _ _	riv _ _	gener _ _	tit _ _
artifici _ _	punctu _ _	norm _ _	vertic _ _	trav _ _
equ _ _	ang _ _	ang _ _		

Here's a little code. Write down the letters of the alphabet, numbering them from 1 to 26. Write in your notebook the words that correspond to:

13, 21, 19, 9, 3, 1, 12;   13, 21, 19, 3, 12, 5;   3, 18, 9, 13, 9, 14, 1, 12;
6, 9, 14, 1, 12;   9, 4, 5, 14, 20, 9, 3, 1, 12;   14, 1, 20, 9, 15, 14, 1, 12;
16, 15, 19, 19, 9, 2, 12, 5;   20, 15, 23, 5, 12;   18, 5, 19, 5, 13, 2, 12, 5;
3, 15, 13, 16, 5, 12.

Bicycle parts crossword

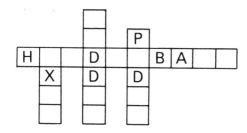

Look in your dictionary to find the difference between

duel, dual   **principle, principal**   **medal, meddle**

16 i before e

i before e, except after c, whenever the sound you are making is **eee**!

i before e

thief	believe	niece	relief
achieve	brief	piece	retrieve

except after c

receive	deceive	ceiling	conceit
conceive	perceive	receipt	deceit

whenever the sound you are making is eee!

shield	conceited	grief	deceitful

Remember that **ie** may make other sounds beside **eee**. Say these words out loud and learn them. Write them in your Spelling Dictionary.

lieutenant	friendship	science	efficient
variety	piercing	barrier	fierce
groceries	denied	patient	sieve

In the same way, **ei** may make other sounds besides **eee**. Say these words out loud and learn them. Write them in your Spelling Dictionary.

eight	foreign	height	forfeit
leisure	weight	being	weir
weird	counterfeit	sovereign	eiderdown

Often **ei** sounds like a long **a**:

neighbour	reign	reins	vein
veil	reindeer	weigh	sleigh

Copy these words into your Spelling Dictionary, filling in the spaces with **ie** or **ei**. Say the words out loud before you fill in the space.

bel __ vable	conc __ ted	consc __ nce	rec __ ving
th __ r	ach __ vement	dec __ t	w __ ghing
s __ zing	misch __ vous	sc __ ntific	conven __ nt
suffic __ nt	pat __ nce	for __ gner	f __ rcely

17 Silent **e** dropped

This rule is about words that end with an **e** which is not pronounced, such as   separate   continue   excite   expense

With such words, you must leave off the final **e** if you want to add an ending that begins with a vowel, such as **-ing** or **-er**:

separate, separation   continue, continually   become, becoming
suppose, supposing   freeze, freezer   use, user, using

Add **-ing** to these words. Write them in your Spelling Dictionary.

argue   judge   amaze   encourage   move
improve   arrange   advertise   amuse   surprise

Add **-ous** or **-able** to these words. Write them in your Dictionary.

fame   adventure   value   ridicule   recognise

18 Silent **e** kept

With words ending in a silent **e**, do not leave off the **e** if you want to add an ending that begins with a consonant.

definite, definitely   sincere, sincerely   move, movement
amuse, amusement   love, lovely   use, useful, useless

There are a few exceptions that need to be learnt:

argue, argument   hate, hatred   true, truly   nine, ninth

Unscramble the words in green (they all end with **e**) to fit the definitions:

veersitda – make known, publicise   urage   – disagree
attse   – declare   oepmirv – get better
earrnga   – put in order; organise   cvheeia – accomplish

Now add **-ment** to all of them and write them in your Spelling Dictionary.

Add **-ness** and **-ly** to these words:

fierce   close   strange   late   rude   sure

19 Shortened words

Some common words, such as **not** and **will**, are shortened both in speaking and in writing. For example, instead of **I do not** and **he will** we may say and write **I don't** and **he'll**. You will see that two words (**do-not** and **he-will**) are joined, and the missing letter or letters replaced by an apostrophe (').

Study these lists carefully and note specially where the apostrophe goes.

1 **not** — isn't   aren't   doesn't   haven't

    There are three special cases:

    will not becomes **won't**   **shall not** becomes **shan't**
    cannot becomes **can't** (with only one **n**)

2 **will** and **shall** — I'll   we'll   they'll   who'll

    The apostrophe replaces more than one letter in these cases. Which letters?

3 **had** and **would** — I'd   we'd   they'd   you'd

    The same form of shortening (**'d**) stands for both **had** and **would**.

4 **are** — we're   you're   they're

5 **have** — I've   we've   they've

6 **is** and **has** — he's   that's   here's

7 **am** — I'm

You must learn the difference between **it's** (meaning **it is**) and **its** (**of it**). How can you remember this?

Write down the shortened forms of these:

did not	what is	she will	who is	who has	it is
it has	has not	who are	you have	he had	he would
you will	was not	she is	could not	would not	who had

20 Prefixes

A prefix is a group of letters, usually one syllable, added to the beginning of a word to change its meaning.

The prefix **in-** or **im-** can mean **not**
   in + visible = invisible = not visible
   im + possible = impossible = not possible

The prefix **re-** can mean **again** or **back**
   re + gain = regain = gain back

The prefix **sub-** usually means **under**
   sub + way = subway = passage under the roadway.

Put one of these prefixes in front of each word. Learn the completed word and write it in your Spelling Dictionary.

capture	join	trace	patient	capable
divide	place	marine	appear	polite
pay	expensive	standard	play	perfect
accurate	merge	frequent	sufficient	fund

Other prefixes include **un-** meaning **not**, and **ex-** meaning **out of** or **from**:

unattractive	unconscious	unnecessary	expense	excursion
unbalance	unfriendly	unlikely	exchange	expel
unbeaten	unfortunate	unselfish	explain	excuse
uncertain	ungrateful	unpleasant	expand	expedition

The **ex-** at the beginning of a word sometimes sounds like **eggs**:

exact	exhausted	exhibit	example	exasperate
exaggerate	examine	exempt	exert	exhilarating

No words that you are likely to use (except **eggshell**) begin with **eggs** or **egs**, so if the beginning of a word sounds like **eggs**, it's safe to assume that it's spelt with **ex-**.

Write down **ex-** words meaning   and **un-** words meaning

1 blow up	4 take out	1 not lived in	4 without help
2 speak out	5 put out	2 boring	5 in two minds
3 stretch out	6 dig out	3 reluctant	6 surprising

21 Words ending in **-ce**, **-ge** and **-ie**

These words follow the main rules you have already learnt for words ending with a silent **e**.

You drop the final **e** if you want to add **-ing**, **-er**, or **-y**:

force, forcing   mince, mincer   ice, icy   fleece, fleecy

You keep the final **e** if you want to add an ending that begins with a consonant:

grace, graceful   large, largely   encourage, encouragement
strange, strangeness

However, you must not drop the **e** if you want to add **-ous** or **-able**:

courage, courageous   notice, noticeable

Notice that words ending in **-ce** drop the **e** before **-tion**:

reduce, reduction   introduce, introduction   produce, production

Words ending in **-ie** change the **ie** into **y** if you add **-ing**:

die, dying   lie, lying   untie, untying

Now add **-ous** or **-able** to

change   peace   outrage

Add **-ing** to

produce   dance   charge   change   reduce   tie
notice   ice   encourage

Complete these words by filling the gaps. Learn the words and write them in your Spelling Dictionary.

At the entran_e was a noti_e that gro_eries and other produ_e were redu_ed in pri_e by ten per _ent.

Use your dictionary to find out the difference between

cereal, serial   colonel, kernel   coarse, course

22   Problems with l

You may wish to add the endings **-ed**, **-ing** or **-er** to a word:

murmur, murmured, murmuring   develop, developer, developing

You may do this with words ending in **-l**:

reveal, revealed, revealing   crawl, crawled, crawling, crawler

But if the final **-l** has a *single* vowel in front of it, you must double the **-l** before adding **-ed**, **-ing**, or **-er**.

cancel, cancelled, cancelling   compel, compelled, compelling
control, controller, controlling   rebel, rebelled, rebelling
total, totalled, totalling   travel, traveller, travelled

Notice that the **-l** is not doubled in the following words, because it does not have a single vowel in front of it; it has a double vowel or a consonant.

cool, cooled, cooling   growl, growled, growling   boil, boiler, boiled

The final **-l** is, however, always doubled if you want to add **-y**.

annually   usually   actually   practically   normally

It is not doubled if you want to add other endings:

rivalry   journalist   usefulness   realistic   perilous
novelist   novelty   originality   fulfilment   loyalty

There are a few exceptions that have to be learnt:

cancel, cancellation   dial, dialled, dialling   oil, oily
cruel, crueller (but cruelty)   instal, instalment   wool, woollen
rebel, rebellion   marvel, marvellous

Words ending in **-ll** never double the final **-l**.

Add **-ed** and **-ing** to

appal   fail   expel   fulfil   equal   snarl
pedal   spoil   enrol   roll   shovel   wail

Add **-ity** and **-y** to

brutal   special   real   mental   local   cordial

23 bb, ff and ll

Here are some common words with -bb-:

stubborn   **jabber**   **robbery**   **ribbon**   **rubbish**   **shabby**

Write in your Spelling Dictionary words ending in -bble meaning:

1 walk with difficulty
2 eat rapidly
3 take small bites
4 small stone
5 move from side to side unsteadily
6 write carelessly
7 fragments of brick or stone
8 speak quickly and indistinctly
9 quarrel

Words with -ff- include

afford	**difficulty**	**affair**	**traffic**	**suffer**	**shuffle**
insufficient	**affection**	**suffocate**	**office**	**effort**	**toffee**

See if you can unscramble these words. You need to add ff to each one to make a word.

urian   **ats**   **utsy**   **ero**   **enod**   **oece**

Finally, learn these important ll words:

brilliant	**especially**	**million**	**collide**	**illegal**	**collect**
generally	**illness**	**stroll**	**hollow**	**thrilling**	**umbrella**

Try to think of ll words meaning places or things where you could keep

1 money
2 paintings
3 air
4 stamps

Use your dictionary to decide whether there should be l or ll in

para _ e _   **de _ iver**   **de _ iberate**   **fo _ owing**
a _ ways   **swo _ en**   **a _ though**   **a _ together**

24 **mm**, **rr** and **tt**

Remember -**mm**- in

command	mummy	recommend	comment
glimmer	common	immense	stammer
immediate	simmer	summit	programme

Make the following changes to some of the above words to make them fit the meanings in the brackets:

1 take away the last two letters (a punctuation mark)
2 add a w (a person who swims)
3 change the last two letters to er (one of the seasons)
4 take away the last letter and add ce (start)
5 change the first letter to d (model of a person)
6 change the first letter to s (less fat)

Don't forget -**rr**- in

arrest	correspond	horrified	furry
sorrow	quarry	arrive	borrow
surrender	irritate	narrow	currency

Don't forget -**tt**- in

| pattern | motto | settle | glitter | cottage | bottom |
| battery | scattered | inattentive | shuttle | tattered | stutter |

Write in your Spelling Dictionary words beginning **att**- meaning

1 join, fasten
2 assault
3 try
4 very pleasant to look at
5 be present

If you have learnt the words in this unit, you should now be able to spell

| immediately | arrival | settler | irritation |
| corresponding | sorry | horror | attentive |

25 Endings in -ful and -less

Although **full** is spolt with two **l**s, if you add it to the end of a word you must always shorten it to -**ful**:

truth, truthful   fear, fearful   cheer, cheerful

The same is true of words ending in -**e**:

taste, tasteful   hope, hopeful   tune, tuneful

Remember two earlier rules:
Words ending in a consonant + **y** change the **y** into **i** before an ending that starts with a consonant:

beauty, beautiful

Words ending in a vowel + **y** keep the **y** before an ending that starts with a consonant:

play, playful

If you want to add -**fully**, there are always two **l**s:

truthful, truthfully   fear, fearfully   cheerful, cheerfully
hopeful, hopefully   tuneful, tunefully   beautiful, beautifully
tasteful, tastefully   playful, playfully   thoughtful, thoughtfully

There are two exceptions you must try to remember:

skill, skilful, skilfully (but skilled)
will, wilful, wilfully (but willed, willing)

If you want to add -**less** or -**lessly**, there are always two **ss**:

fearless, fearlessly   hopeless, hopelessly   tasteless, tastelessly
thoughtless, thoughtlessly

If you **hope**, you are **hopeful**. What are you if you

| think | doubt | waste | thank | succeed | hate |
| regret | forget | boast | help | deceive | pity |

Write in your Spelling Dictionary words ending in -**ful** and -**fully** made from

delight   skill   spite   joy   peace   mercy   dread

26 -ent and -ence

Learn these words. Do you understand what they all mean?

absent, absence	urgent	student	conscience
different, difference	incident	accident	sentence
silent, silence	parent	opponent	influence

Change each of the following words to end in **-ence**. Write both words in your Spelling Dictionary.

innocent   confident   patient   excellent   obedient   violent

Change each of the following words to end in **-ent**. Write both words in your Spelling Dictionary.

negligence   evidence   independence   residence   prominence

Write in your Spelling Dictionary the words that are opposite in meaning to

absence	defence	absent	convenient	intelligent	convenience
efficient	frequent	ascent	patience	obedient	

It is important to memorise a few words that end in **-ense**:

sense   dense   nonsense   expense   tense   suspense

27 -able and -ible

These endings sound alike. It's important to learn the difference in spelling.

unmistakable	comfortable	dependable	lovable	miserable
usable	reliable	reasonable	valuable	liable
respectable	perishable	probable	vegetable	portable
noticeable	changeable	remarkable	knowledgeable	unbreakable

The **-ible** ending is less common:

horrible   incredible   sensible   edible   terrible   flexible

Remember to drop the **-e** if you want to add **-y**:

comfortably   reasonably   possibly   horribly   terribly   miserably

Write out the opposites of

visible   possible   desirable   responsible   illegible

28 Silent letters

Some English words have letters which are not pronounced. There are no rules to help you; you just have to learn the words. Here are some of the most common ones.

Silent b

bomb	numb	dumb	plumber	tomb	thumb
climb	crumb	debt	doubt	limb	comb

Silent k (in kn, usually at the beginning of words)

knowledge	knock	knitting	knot	knife	knob
knee	knead	kneel	knuckle	knack	knapsack

Silent u

biscuit	guarantee	guess	circuit	guard	guitar
tongue	building	fatigue	guilty	guide	catalogue

Silent t

fasten	moisten	often	soften	christening	listen
rustle	bristle	bustle	jostle	whistle	nestle

Silent c

science	scene	scissors	descent	discipline	scythe
conscious	except	excellent	excitement	exceed	excess

Silent h

honest	honour	hour	heir (heiress)	honorary

Silent i

suitable	juice	pursuit	bruise	fruitful

Silent n

column	autumn	condemn	hymn	solemn

Silent w (mainly in wr, and at the beginning of words)

write	wrap	wrist	wrench	wrong	wreck
wreath	wretched	wrestle	wriggle	wrinkle	sword

29 Words with **pp**, **cc** and **dd**

It's often difficult to know whether to use one **p** or two. Here are some common words with **-pp-** for you to learn.

appear	supply	oppose	supporter	appetite
apply	appreciate	opportunity	approve	suppose
slippery	applaud	happiness	approximately	opposite

Remember that **cc** sounds like **ks** in

accept	accident	accent	accelerate	succeed	eccentric

but **cc** sounds like **k** in

accuse	accurate	account	occupy	accompany	according

Try specially hard to remember two of the most commonly mis-spelt words in English: **accommodation**   **occasionally**

Finally, here are some popular **dd** words.

address	sudden	wedding	paddling	pudding	shudder

Write in your Spelling Dictionary any other **pp**, **cc** and **dd** words that you can think of.

If you have learnt the words on this page, you should be able to spell these words, too:

opposition	approval	occasion	suddenly
accidental	supplies	addressed	accuracy

Puzzle corner

Complete the boxes to make words meaning

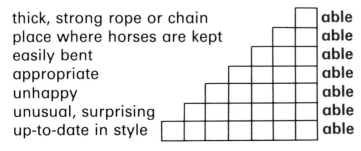

thick, strong rope or chain — able
place where horses are kept — able
easily bent — able
appropriate — able
unhappy — able
unusual, surprising — able
up-to-date in style — able

30 Words beginning **dis-** and **des-**

Look at these words and learn them.

discover	discuss	disgust	dismal	disease
distract	dissolve	district	disturb	distinct
disappointed	disperse	display	distribute	distinguish

dis- can be added to the beginning of a word to make it opposite in meaning.

dis + obey = disobey = opposite of obey

displease	dismount	disadvantage	discontinue
disappear	disapproval	disbelieve	discomfort
disqualify	discontent	dishearten	dissatisfied

des- is a less common beginning

describe	desert	deserve	desire	despair
desperate	despise	destination	destroy	despite

Some of these words sound as if they should be spelt **diz-**. Which ones? No words you are likely to use begin with **diz-** (except **dizzy** and **dizziness**), so if a first syllable sounds like **diz-**, assume that it is spelt **dis-** or **des-**.

There are ten **dis-** words in the box. They are printed across, down, backwards, upside-down, or diagonally. Find them, learn them, and write them in your Spelling Dictionary.

D	I	S	P	A	I	R	E	S	I	D
R	I	L	S	I	D	K	A	A	D	E
I	E	S	D	I	I	D	S	S	I	E
T	P	T	I	L	S	I	S	I	S	R
S	N	E	S	O	P	S	I	D	L	G
U	I	I	T	A	S	A	M	I	O	A
R	D	M	A	I	S	S	S	S	Y	S
T	I	I	N	I	D	I	I	I	A	I
S	R	E	C	O	S	I	D	D	L	D
I	I	D	E	D	I	S	P	U	T	E
D	R	E	D	R	O	S	I	D	I	S

Make sure you know the difference between desert with the stress on the first syllable
and desert with the stress on the last syllable.
What does dessert mean?

31 Words with **ph**

ph sounds like **f** in some words:

at the beginning	photo phone	physical phantom	phrase pharmacy
in the middle	alphabet nephew	atmosphere pamphlet	typhoon emphasise
at the end	triumph	graph	epitaph
but not always!	shepherd	uphold	upholstery

Write words ending in **-phone** meaning

1 musical instrument you play with sticks
2 musical instrument you blow into
3 equipment for talking to someone distant
4 equipment for helping to make the voice louder

Write words beginning or ending in **graph** meaning

1 a person's signature
2 vivid
3 a picture taken by a camera
4 a group of sentences

Follow the lines to make words meaning

1 place for children with no parents
2 an animal
3 a bird
4 something round
5 a disaster
6 a piece of music
7 a piece of punctuation
8 half of 4
9 a person's own life-story
10 a study of the earth's surface

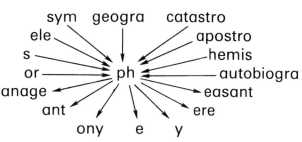

Write the words in your Spelling Dictionary.

32 Endings in **-tion** and **-sion**

Look at these words and learn them.

obligation	preparation	superstition	intention
destruction	operation	investigation	position
section	foundation	caution	condition
exhaustion	repetition	education	conversation
motion	revolution	exaggeration	invention
reputation	junction	concentration	station

The ending **-sion** is less common.

collision	vision	invasion	discussion	passion
conclusion	illusion	explosion	extension	impression
provision	mansion	expansion	confusion	tension

There are a few words with endings that sound the same as **-tion** and **-sion**, but their spellings are different:

fashion	ocean	complexion	musician	cushion
optician	magician	suspicion	politician	electrician

Write out the full words in your Spelling Dictionary. The first one is done for you.

+ = addition
! = ex _ _ _ _ _ _ _ _
½ = frac _ _ _ _

÷ = div _ _ _ _ _
− = sub _ _ _ _ _ _ _ _
a = b = equa _ _ _ _

? = qu _ _ _ _ _ _
× = mul _ _ _ _ _ _ _ _ _ _

If people **oppose**, they give **opposition**. Write down what they give if they

direct	decide	appreciate	subscribe	apply
recognise	explain	celebrate	express	admire
imitate	introduce	permit	describe	persuade
congratulate	satisfy	inspire	console	contribute

Fill in the blank spaces:

In the **exam** _ _ _ _ _ _ _ we had to find the **solu** _ _ _ _ to several **calcu** _ _ _ _ _ _ _. If we had paid more **att** _ _ _ _ _ _ to our **revi** _ _ _ _. there would not have been so much **confu** _ _ _ _ and **depre** _ _ _ _ _ _.